The Bald Eagles of Money Bayou

An Almost True Story

Photographs & Story by

Valerie Seyforth Clayton

THE BALD EAGLES OF MONEY BAYOU
An Almost True Story
Copyright ©2019 by Valerie Seyforth Clayton

Photographs taken by Valerie Seyforth Clayton
"Dottiewoods" photo on page 8 and Watcher photo on page 3 were taken by Dorothy Rogers
Photo on Page 17 taken by Karyl Gavigan

Direct inquiries to:
MiracleofMB@gmail.com

Cover & Interior Design by Ampersand Book Interiors

ISBN: 978-0-578-60466-4

Printed in the United States of America
First Edition November 2019

This book is dedicated to

Dorothy Jean Taylor Rogers

"Dottie"

who protects all God's Creatures

Once upon a time,

a pair of bald eagles named Jack and Elizabeth lived in a

land called Money Bayou, where pirates once roamed.

There,

the two built a large

nest in the highest pine tree in the area called Dottiewoods.

They were beautiful eagles with white heads and tails that

glistened in the Florida sun. With their large yellow talons

and beaks, they hunted for fish in the nearby Gulf of

Mexico waters.

2

The Guardian, a wise lady with bright blue eyes, lived there as well with her black dog Sootie. From her deck, she protected the eagles from all intruders.

Many days the Watcher came to the nest to see the eagles,

and she became friends with the Guardian.

They both loved to watch the eagles.

Over the years, the eagle couple raised many eaglets. Each year when the babies were grown, they flew away to other lands. Jack and Elizabeth would then fly away on summer vacation, knowing their job was well done.

One year, late in the summer, Jack and Elizabeth returned and worked on their nest. They worked many long days in the Florida heat, performing nest-orations, as they precisely placed the twigs and grass in their nest.

4

When work was completed each day, they rested on a perch in a tree near the beach and watched the children play in the sand.

In the evenings, they waited patiently to catch fish for dinner in the warm Gulf waters.

One October day, Jack and Elizabeth sensed something was changing in the weather. They watched the Guardian as she boarded up the windows on her house and noticed her eyes were full of concern. The Guardian knew that a strong hurricane named Michael was approaching their beautiful land. She called to the eagles and begged them to leave.

As the winds became stronger, the Guardian looked toward the nest with sadness. She left Dottiewoods and sought refuge in a safe place miles away. Jack and Elizabeth knew they had to leave as well, and high above the storm, the eagle couple flew to escape the mighty winds.

The water raged over the dunes of the white beach, as the hurricane roared over the land of Money Bayou. The tremendous winds blew and blew until the nest tree crashed to the ground.

The next day, when all was calm, the Guardian knew she must return to her home. With the help of friends and chainsaws, they cut through downed trees and made a path to her home. Dottiewoods was a mess!

With tears in her eyes, the Guardian looked at her destroyed land, and then she remembered the nest. As she looked to where the nest tree had been, she saw it was gone! She scanned the area with her eyes, and there the tree lay with the nest in pieces! Sadness overcame her, but the cleanup must begin.

9

As the neighborhood residents joined together to clean what they could, tractors and dump trucks hauled away tons of trees and rubble. While they worked, the Guardian wondered what happened to her precious eagle pair.

A few days later,

while having morning coffee on her deck, Sootie barked.

The Guardian looked up and much to her surprise, the eagle couple called to each other as they soared to a new tree!

She watched as they brought twigs and sticks to build a new nest. For days, the eagles placed each stick carefully until the nest was complete.

On New Year's Day, Elizabeth called Jack to the nest and surprised him with an egg surrounded by soft grasses and tucked safely in the bowl of the nest.

For the next month, the couple took turns sitting in the nest, incubating and protecting the egg.

Jack would guard the nest from a nearby tree. He would bring Elizabeth new nesting materials and fish for food. As they sat on the egg, their warm feathers protected it from the winter cold and wind.

At the beginning of February, the Guardian heard soft cheeps from the nest. A new eaglet had hatched!

The Watcher came to see the new little one. As they peered at the nest, the Watcher exclaimed that the eaglet was a miracle! The eaglet now had a name.

Both Jack and Elizabeth shared the duties of feeding and protecting the little one.

Miracle grew rapidly.

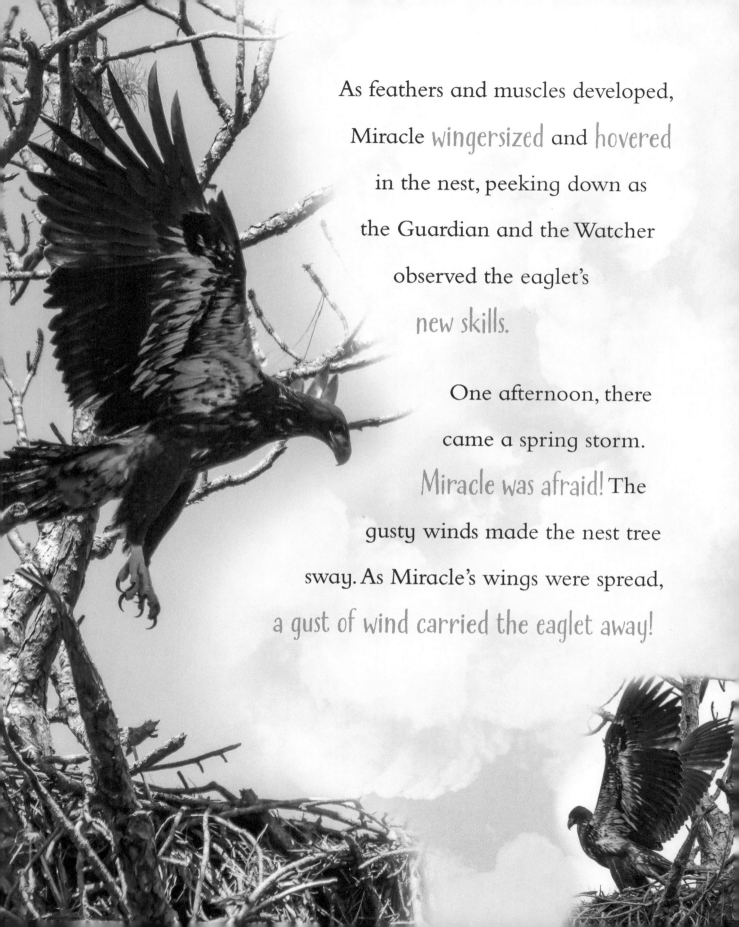

As feathers and muscles developed, Miracle wingersized and hovered in the nest, peeking down as the Guardian and the Watcher observed the eaglet's new skills.

One afternoon, there came a spring storm. Miracle was afraid! The gusty winds made the nest tree sway. As Miracle's wings were spread, a gust of wind carried the eaglet away!

The next morning, the Guardian looked toward the nest tree. Miracle was gone! Worried, the Guardian phoned the Watcher of the nest, since she was wise in the way of eagles. She would know what to do! The Watcher took the Guardian's snake stick and climbed

a fence that surrounded

the area. She searched

for Miracle at the

base of the tree.

When she finally

made it to the

tree, sadness

overcame her.

Miracle was

nowhere to be

found.

One morning,

a few days later, the Guardian worked in her **beautiful yard** full of April flowers with Sootie by her side. She worried but hoped Miracle was somewhere **safe**. Jack and Elizabeth had disappeared as well, but perhaps they were **caring for Miracle** elsewhere.

As the Guardian tended to her garden, Sootie began to
look to the sky. Miracle appeared awkwardly flying, and
close behind the eaglet were Jack and Elizabeth. They were
carefully guiding Miracle to the nest.

Upon returning

to the nest, Miracle began to show independence from

Jack and Elizabeth by hop jumping in the nest, branching

in the nest tree, and taking short

flights to nearby

trees.

The eaglet had become a fledgling! By watching parents carefully, Miracle learned to hunt and fish by trial and error.

A new challenge
arose one day, as a
mockingbird invaded
the neighborhood. The

pesky bird flew all around Jack and Miracle. Jack ignored
the bird as it flew around him.

Miracle, now the size of an adult eagle, was annoyed at the
mockingbird's attacks. The
mockingbird perched
boldly on the limb with
Miracle as they stared
each other down.

Tired of the mockingbird's taunting, in one quick motion,

Miracle turned and gave a mighty poop squirt

at the little pest! The mockingbird left and returned no more.

At last, Miracle had learned all the skills needed for survival, and it was time to leave Money Bayou. As the Guardian watched, Miracle jumped from the perch tree and soared to the sky!

Beautiful dark brown feathers covered the strong eagle's body. Miracle was now a juvenile bald eagle and ready to see the world! Jack flew closely near Miracle as they headed north. Flying away, Miracle looked back and nodded thanks to the Guardian who watched until she could see them no more.

A few days later,

Jack returned to Dottiewoods where Elizabeth sat on a perch in their favorite tree. Jack softly pecked a kiss on Elizabeth's cheek. The couple knew that, once again,

their job was well done.

Thank You,

Miracle

Karen Minger, Media Specialist at Port St. Joe Elementary, who encouraged me to write this book

Dorothy "Dottie" Rodgers who has allowed me to monitor and take photographs of this bald eagle nest

and her dog Sootie who alerts us all as the eagles fly in and out of the area

Kathy Brantley for sharing her view of the nest so many awesome photographs could be taken

Shawnlei Breeding, Audubon EagleWatch Program Manager,

and Lynda Flynn White, former Audubon EagleWatch Coordinator, for Florida bald eagle education

Jack & Elizabeth

Dawn Lee McKenna, author of The Forgotten Coast Florida Suspense and The Still Waters Suspense Series, for being an inspiration

My sister, Karyl Seyforth Gavigan, who helped me brainstorm this book as well as edit

My mother, Caroline Seyforth, who taught me the love of reading and helped edit

My dad, Fred Seyforth, who takes long rides with me to the eagle nests with my Golden doodle Gracie

Carmel Dodson, my friend, who has taught me many photographer skills as we take photographs together

My son, Austin Clayton, who loves his "crazy eagle lady" momma

My students, at Port St. Joe Elementary, who share my love of eagles

About the author

Valerie Seyforth Clayton lives in the Panhandle of Florida. With 32 years of teaching experience, to instill a love of animals, she encourages her elementary technology students to watch live animal cams. While watching the Southwest Florida Eagle Cam during chemotherapy for breast cancer in 2016–17, she began an interest in bald eagles. Currently in her spare time, she takes photographs and monitors bald eagle nests for the Florida Audubon EagleWatch Program.

CPSIA information can be obtained
at www.ICGtesting.com
Printed in the USA
LVHW072224221119
638245LV00004B/43/P